and
Meryl-Lynn
Pluck

Warts Need ACTION

Illustrated by
Evan Lole

TOXIC

For a very long time, I've had a wart on my foot and a wart on my thumb, not to mention the wart on my knee and the wart on my … never you mind.

"Mum," I say, "I know you said I'd grow out of these warts if I was patient. I don't mind too much the warts on my foot, knee and thumb but I just can't stand any longer the wart on my …"

"Maybe," says my mum, "it's time for the Dandelion Weed Remedy. Go into the garden and pick a dandelion. Squeeze the milky white juice from the stalk onto your warts. Do this twice a day and the warts will disappear in a week."

After two weeks of squeezing the milk from the dandelion onto my warts twice a day I still have warts … a wart on my foot and a wart on my knee. I still have a wart on my thumb and worst of all I still have the wart on my …

"What you need," says my dad, "is a potato… a white potato; not one that's started to sprout, mind, because they're poisonous.

"Cut the potato in half, leaving the skin on. Rub one half of the potato all over your warts.

"Take this half potato outside and bury it in the dirt where no one will find it. Throw away the other half potato.

"So long as you don't tell anyone what you've done, your warts will disappear in five days."

I do exactly as my dad tells me and I wait five days. Nothing happens.

"Steve," I say to our neighbour. "Have you ever had warts?"

"Yes," says Steve. "Most kids get them and their mothers tell them they'll grow out of them. It doesn't happen quickly enough for most kids. Warts need action.

"Find yourself a common house brick and a chain off a motorbike. Attach the brick to the wart by fixing it in place using the motorbike chain. Do this ten minutes a day for a fortnight and the wart will be gone."

I follow Steve's instructions. For ten minutes of every day for the next two weeks I attach a brick to my warts, using the motorbike chain.

There's no change at all but on the fourteenth day my grandma pays a surprise visit. She sees me with the brick and chain attached. "What on earth are you doing with a brick attached to THERE with a motorbike chain?"

"I've got problems with warts," I tell my grandma.

"Look." I show her the wart on my foot and the wart on my thumb. I show her the wart on my knee.

"That's quite enough," she says. "I get the picture! Banana peel is the best cure for warts. Here, eat this banana and save the peel. Cut the peel into pieces and put one on each wart, using this tape. The skin will go black and mushy and on the tenth day the warts will be gone."

I believe it worth a try and I get Grandma to help me to cover the wart on my foot and the wart on my thumb. She helps me cover the wart on my knee but I do the other one myself.

Just as Grandma says, the banana skin turns black and mushy. What she didn't mention was the stink! On the tenth day I remove the tape and the stinky, mushy, black banana skin. No luck; the warts are still there. If I'd been paying for these remedies I'd be asking for my money back!

I decide it's time to consult the experts at school. It seems everyone has a remedy for warts and I try covering my warts with sand, then lime juice.

I try baking soda and vinegar but I think that expert got confused with making a volcano!

I apply raw garlic, toothpaste and raw bacon to my warts. One expert convinces me to eat raw cabbage (yuk!) and another advises me to cover my warts with cooked cabbage.

Nothing works until the day my dad's crazy brother, my favourite uncle, comes to visit.

"The best way to get rid of warts is to get someone to buy them off you," he says.

I decide one more silly game can't hurt and I say, "I'll take payment for the wart on my foot and the wart on my thumb. I'll take payment for the wart on my knee and I'll throw in for free the wart on my …"

"It's a deal," says my uncle, handing over a handful of coins.

And believe it or not, that was the last I saw of my warts … I am free of the wart on my foot and the wart on my thumb. I am free of the wart on my knee and best of all I no longer have a wart on my …

… tum!